CONTENTS

Written by Luke Gearing.

Illustrated by David Hoskins.

Editing & Development by Jarrett Crader. ⚘

Layout & Development by Christian Kessler. ⚘

Proofreading by Fiona Maeve Geist. ⚘

Deluxe PDF by Corey Brin. ⚘

Additional Proofreading by Alexander Saify

ACID
DEATH
FANTASY

LUKE GEARING

Introduction

WHAT HAPPENED is long forgotten. Remains of it, barely understood by the most learned scholars, are rife throughout the lands but most are too busy surviving or maintaining their strangleholds on WATER and POWER, POWER and WATER to ponder these RELICS.

The greatest living city of the desert is *Shurupak,* breeding ground of pleasure and nightmare. All people, all faiths, all goods are valued in meretricious Shurupak, ruled by the **Many-Crowned Monarch** and her terrible guard a thousand-thousand strong. The wealth of the city is untouched, uncontested, and many covet the throne. The **Many-Crowned Monarch**—bestudded by ninety-nine crowns wrested by all manner of statecraft and violence—rules as gatekeeper to a warren of gluttony and civilization. Each of her heads has a tale and a crown.

Spinning outwards from *Shurupak* are the *Thousand Sultanates,* a great miscellany of egotism, pride and petty squabbles. There is much wealth-the titles of these many pretenders are not entirely false. They compete endlessly in petty games, inevitably forgotten as the hubris of the current ruler inevitably causes a fall. Those closest to *Shurupak,* (*Alshgar the Nightmare Emirate,* the *Beggar Sultanate* and the *Valley of Wisdom* to name but a few) are the most ancient and stablest whilst the peripheral Emirs and Maliks barely maintain their grasp for a generation or more.

Beyond this anarchic sprawl are the *Wastes*—lands riddled with all manner of nomadic groups and beasts dwelling beneath the sands, all bowing in respect to the WORMS roaming freely atwixt the dunes. The **Alqai,** four armed metal-workers, emerge from the Duneholds to sell exquisitely worked goods or continue the ages-old war with the **Dune Riders** on their slender sand-slicing boats.

The *Southern Wastes* are the home of the Sᴌᴏᴜɢʜ Lɪᴢᴀʀᴅʟɪɴɢs, a brutal, reptilian species that leaves the butchered limbs of their prey scattered in artful piles across the desert, maimed survivors remaining as testament to their art, baking in the sun like tortoises dropped by eagles.

To the East lies the *Plastic Sea,* a miraculous main of liquid plastic. Upon contact with living skin it solidifies, covering the coast with **Coated Men** dueling each other in elegant, fatal contests, having made the choice to die young and glorious, sealed in flexible plastic armour.

The verdant jungles of the North would offer respite from the desert if not for the patriarchal **Azure Apes.** Whilst the stable nests happily accept visitors, the zones between are haunted by failed alpha-males who gladly prey upon travellers to strengthen themselves for challenges against aging nest-masters. Not even these desperate beasts dare try themselves against the shining, metallic ruins scattered throughout the jungle.

To the West is the graveyard of the Oʟᴅ Gods whose steel skeletons loom over a great and terrible *Rubble.* Once a city of the gods' chosen peoples, their undoing was terrible, their grey stone, unknown to us, remains a mystery.

PC Backgrounds
11 Wasteland Wanderer
You hail from the wastes or a less-powerful sultanate. You were raised eating snake eggs and worshipping spirits. You might have been nomadic or settled in a village. You distrust city folk for their wicked ways, and may covet their wealth and luxury. You might be the last survivor of your people, forever destined to wander.

POSSESSIONS
- *4 SPEARS.*
- *4 EXTRA PROVISIONS.*
- *A SHIELD.*
- *A LUCK TOTEM* (may be used in place of a Luck point once per week).

ADVANCED SKILLS
3 Trapping
3 Foraging
2 Spear Fighting
2 Awareness

12 Shaved Bear
In the mountains near the Plastic Sea are the few remaining nihilistic, anti-natalist, monastic Bear Men who spend their days meditating on nothingness and extinction. You've rejected this philosophy, shaved yourself to brave the heat of the desert, and descended to engage in the madness of the wastes, pulsing with life and hope. You are rare but not unknown.

POSSESSIONS
- *LARGE BAG OF SHAVED HAIR.*
- *CLAWS* (Damage as Sword).

ADVANCED SKILLS
5 Strength
3 Claw Fighting
2 Philosophy

13 Alqai

Beneath the sands your people toil, digging out shards of metal of some long forgotten war. You're stout, wrapped about with a shell like an armadillo, and have four arms. The life of toil and war without the sun left you wanting and so you set out.

POSSESSIONS
- *SHELL* (as Modest Armour).
- *2 MACES.*
- *2 MORE MACES OR 2 SHIELDS.*

ADVANCED SKILLS
3 Smithing
3 Metallurgy
2 Mace Fighting
2 Sneak

SPECIAL
You've got four arms.

14 Dune Rider

You were an outrider of your fleet, a three-armed, no-legged scout, guiding the fleet away from danger and towards vulnerable targets. Something happened and you left, perhaps by choice. You still have your single-rider craft but you've lost your purpose.

POSSESSIONS
- *ONE-MAN DUNE RIDER CRAFT* (twice as fast as a horse, Roll Under for use in harsh weather, only usable in the desert).
- *DUNE RIDER SICKLE* (Damage as Axe while on foot or as Polearm when riding your craft & charging).
- *A MEMENTO OF HOME.*

ADVANCED SKILLS
4 Dune Riding
3 Navigation
2 Sickle Fighting

SPECIAL
You have 3 Multi-Purpose Limbs. You need at least two free to walk in an ungainly manner.

15 Rebel Azure Ape

You were a Queen, content in the nest of your alpha in the jungles of the North, then you learned of freedom, adventure, and choice. You gathered your children and set off.

POSSESSIONS
- *3 BABY AZURE APES* (Skill 4, Stamina 5, Damage as Small Beasts).

ADVANCED SKILLS
3 Strength
2 Foraging
2 Healing

SPECIAL
You must provide your babies with one Provision between the three of them each day. After a year, they mature.

16 Sultanless Guard

You were once a feared and respected person, a guardian to one of the many sultans of the wastes. As always, the sultanate fell, leaving you cast adrift on the currents of the world, seeking fortune or purpose.

POSSESSIONS
- *1 PRIMARY WEAPON*.
- *1 SECONDARY WEAPON*.
- *SCALED ARMOUR* (as Modest Armour).
- *LOVE LETTER FROM SOMEONE IN THE FALLEN SULTANATE*.

ADVANCED SKILLS
3 Fighting in your Primary Weapon
3 Etiquette
2 Fighting in your Secondary Weapon
1 Awareness

21 Slough Lizardling

You are one of the anarchist, reptilian murderers of the Southern Wastes, known for horrendous brutality and sculptures made of limbs bound together by cacti-needles. You left your people behind, perhaps seeking to test yourself and return ready to shepard them as a Slough Warlord.

POSSESSIONS
- *POLEARM.*
- *BAG OF CACTI NEEDLES.*
- *LIZARD-SKIN* (as Light Armour).

Advanced Skills
3 Polearm Fighting
3 Art (Limb Sculpture)
1 in any Skill
1 in any Skill
1 in any Skill

SPECIAL

As a reptile you struggle if you cannot bask in the sun or warm yourself before a fire, meaning you only add one Initiative Token to the Stack.

22 Eunuch

You are, or were, a trusted member of a noble house or sultanate, your inability to sire or birth a lineage in the case of a coup increasing the faith they had in you. Why do you wander free? What do you seek?

POSSESSIONS
- SECRET MISSION or A PRICE ON YOUR HEAD.
- FINE CLOTHING.
- FINE DRINK.
- FINE KNIFE (Damage as Polearm).

ADVANCED SKILLS
4 Etiquette
2 Healing
2 Disguise
2 in Any Skill
1 Knife Fighting

23 Life-Rider

The six armed, no-legged, blue-hued Life Riders form unbreakable bonds with their mounts and exist in a heavily mercantile culture. Your mount, chosen at birth, determined your role in the caravan until you struck out, alone. You share the hatred of the Dune-Riders common to all Life-Riders.

POSSESSIONS
- LIFE-MOUNT.
- LANCE (Damage as Spear).
- FORELEG BONES OF THE MOUNT OF YOUR (parent/friend/lover).

ADVANCED SKILLS
3 Riding
2 Lance Fighting
2 Navigation
2 Haggling

SPECIAL
Pick one entry marked * from the Enemies section—this is your Life-Mount. If it dies it cannot be replaced and you suffer -1d6 Luck permanently.

24 Sandworm Rider

You were nobody until you successfully rode the True Lord of the Desert, the Sandworm. You're now something between a shaman and a trouble-shooter. It is true that the Worm showed you things but what mystical properties you ascribe to this is known to only to you.

POSSESSIONS
- WORM-HOOKS.
- SWORD.
- 1D6 POWERLESS CHARMS (+1 to influence the Nomads).
- WORM-DRUMS (attuned to a specific Worm, usable only in the Deep Desert).

ADVANCED SKILLS
2 Spell—Random
2 Spell—Random
2 Astrology
2 Healing

25 Rubble Dweller

You were born and raised in the shadows of dead gods, picking through the endless rubble and debris of a dead age. Oh, what things you have found and lost!

POSSESSIONS
- LASER PISTOL (Damage as Pistolet) or SOLAR POWERED ARMOUR (as Heavy Armour).
- RATTY CLOTHES.
- 1D6 ITEMS OF SENTIMENTAL JUNK or THE LOCATION OF THE SHOES.

ADVANCED SKILLS
2 Sneak
2 Run
2 Scavenging
2 Barter
2 Forage

26 Coated Man

You were one of the many pilgrims who traveled to the Plastic Sea, having chosen glory and young death above being worn down by The Sands. You decided to test yourself in the world at large rather than die upon the Plastic Shores.

POSSESSIONS
- *WEAPON* of your choice.
- *PLASTIC-COATED SKIN* (as Light Armour).
- *DEATH WISH*.

ADVANCED SKILLS
4 Fighting in your chosen Weapon
3 Dodge
2 Artistic Media of your choice
1 in any Advanced Skill

SPECIAL
Your coating kills you, slowly—your maximum age is 40.

31 Coated Squire

You're a hanger-on, a chronicler of desperate fights and a shameless fanboy. You know much of the theory of battle and none of the practicality. You probably yell directions from the side-lines, a lot.

POSSESSIONS
- *1D6 DRAFTS OF CHRONICLES REGARDING COATED MEN.*
- *KNIFE.*
- *CRUDE, HOME-MADE BANNER DEPICTING YOUR FAVOURITE (LIVING) COATED MAN.*

ADVANCED SKILLS
4 Tactics
3 Strategy
2 Etiquette
1 Run

SPECIAL
Once per encounter you may Test Luck on behalf of another. This is you yelling advice. They don't have to follow your advice but they must decide before you roll.

32 Hyenaman Scavenger

As a Hyenaman you have a religious relationship with trash. You are festooned with potentially useful items—if only the right situation came up.

POSSESSIONS
- *EFFECTIVELY UNLIMITED SMALL ITEMS OF NEAR-USELESS CRAP.*
- *SPEAR.*
- *SHIELD.*
- *YOUR FAVOURITE, DEFINITELY USEFUL, PIECE OF TRASH.*

ADVANCED SKILLS
5 Scavenge
3 Run
2 Forage

SPECIAL
Whenever you need a specific item you may Test Luck to dig through your trash pile. Success indicates you have *JUST THE RIGHT ITEM*. You may forgo this Test and use your *FAVOURITE PIECE OF TRASH* but it is gone forever (this includes Weapons, technology, religious and magical artefacts of low power, etc.).

33 Refugee of the Past

You awoke in a glass tube in the midst of the remains of your culture. Everything is gone. You were frozen to restore the Old World—but seeing this desolation, is it worth it?

POSSESSIONS
- *SOLAR-POWERED LASER PISTOL* (Damage as Pistolet, 2d6 uses per day).
- *SURVIVAL KNIFE.*
- *MEMENTO OF LOVED ONES.*

ADVANCED SKILLS
2 Laser Pistol Fighting
1 Knife Fighting
1 Navigation
1 Foraging
1 Survival
1 Ancient History
1 Sneak

34 Narrowman Nomad

You are one of the mysterious, stilt-legged Narrowmen, reputed to have a powerful mysticism. You stand 3 meters tall, towering above the crowds as you seek out seemingly useless, petty items from the bazaars.

POSSESSIONS
- *POLEARM.*
- *HUGE BOW* and *12 ARROWS.*
- *A BLASPHEMOUS IDOL.*

ADVANCED SKILLS
2 Polearm Fighting
2 Bow Fighting
2 Navigation
2 Barter
2 Spell—Random

35 Freshwater Grub Agent

You are, or were, an agent for one of the rare and ruthless Freshwater Grubs, leading their criminal empires from their Aquarium-Thrones filled with precious, filtered water. You've been extensively trained and well paid.

POSSESSIONS
- *A SECRET MISSION* or *HITMEN ON YOUR TAIL*.
- *SELF-CHARGING LASER PISTOL* (Damage as Pistolet, 1d4 uses per day).
- *SHORTSWORD*.
- *DESERT-CLOAK*.
- *FINERY IN A BAG*.
- *DISGUISE KIT*.

ADVANCED SKILLS
3 Disguise
2 Dodge
2 Sneak
1 Laser Pistol Fighting
1 Sword Fighting
1 Run

36 Sand-Sifter

Some make their fortunes in blood, others in knowledge, lore and learning. Some live by their wits. Not you. You have a sieve, patience and a desert.

POSSESSIONS
- *BIT HAT WITH VEIL*.
- *SAND-SIEVE*.
- *INNUMERABLE POCKETS*.

ADVANCED SKILLS
4 Hide
3 Prospecting
2 Run
1 Sand-Fighting

SPECIAL
Per every hour spent sieving you retrieve 1d6 random items from the sand. Many are half-useless, other simply dropped or forgotten, though you know what they say about another person's trash...

41 Sha'ir

You weave words into poetry and spells alike. You are greatly respected by the Thousand Sultans, who often pay heavily to be your patron.

POSSESSIONS
- *UNFINISHED EPIC POEM.*

ADVANCED SKILLS
4 Poetry
2 Spell—Random
2 Spell—Random

42 Retired Gladiator

You've spilt more blood, crushed more skulls, been gouged and bitten by bigger beasts than most. Old stories don't pay the rent, though, and your arms know only one labour.

POSSESSIONS
- *SCARS.*
- *3 WEAPONS* of your choice.
- *MODEST ARMOUR* or *LIGHT ARMOUR AND A NET.*
- *FAMOUS PREVIOUS BOUT* or *ASPIRING PROTEGE.*

ADVANCED SKILLS
3 Fighting of your choice
2 Fighting of your choice
2 Theatrics
2 Strength
1 Fighting of your choice

43 Petty Priest

You are unpopular—religion is not common amongst the peoples of the waste, yet you truly believe. They blessed you with such powers, how could they not be a true god?

POSSESSIONS
- None—**They** will care for you.

ADVANCED SKILLS
3 Spell—Random
3 Spell—Random
3 Spell—Random
1 Preaching

SPECIAL
Construct your deity using the Spells you have been blessed with as cues.

44 Serf

You were a serf in one of the Thousand Sultanates, toiling in the desert and merciless heat only to have the fruit of your sweat snatched away. No more. You stole some arms and armour and set out to seek fortune.

POSSESSIONS
- *A FAMILY RELYING ON THE WEALTH YOU SEND HOME.*
- *STOLEN SWORD.*
- *STOLEN MODEST ARMOUR.*

ADVANCED SKILLS
2 Sword Fighting
2 Dodge
2 Strength
2 Awareness

45 Technician of Esteemed Acquisitions

The wealth of the few should, indeed, be redistributed—to those most able to appreciate the qualities of such fine artefacts—by such redistribution the uplifting qualities of these items are maximised. You are simply an instrument of this natural process. Thievery is profane. Esteemed Acquisition is sublime, and pays better.

POSSESSIONS
- *TORTOISE WITH A CANDLE ON ITS BACK.*
- *ROPE.*
- *ASSORTMENT OF HAND MIRRORS.*
- *PEARL-GRIP SCISSORS.*
- *BEAUTIFUL SILK SCARF WITH RAZOR EDGE* or *DAZZLING LIZARD-SKIN COAT HIDING THROWING KNIVES.*

ADVANCED SKILLS
3 Stealth
2 Climb
1 Scarf Fighting or Knife Fighting

SPECIAL
All technicians carry a Manual of Esteemed Acquisitions, penned by the founder of their School of Esteemed Acquisitions. These detail tenets of the School and a unique scoring matrix for any given Acquisition, as well as instruction in a skill of the Master.

1D6	MANUAL NAME AND AUTHOR	ADVANCED SKILLS
1	THE LURID TECHNIQUES OF THE PERFUMED SMOKE by **Ku-Aya**	3 Poisons 3 Acrobatics
2	THE ACQUISITION OF ESTEEMED SOULS AS RELATED by **Atab the Shrouded**	Add 2 to Fighting Skill of choice Add 2 to Climb 2 Bow
3	REVELATIONS OF MUDTONGUED SINNASHI	4 Breach 2 Second Sight
4	THE ENDLESS CHAIN OF FACES AND LIVES by **Aruru**	3 Disguise 3 Etiquette
5	UPON SHURUPAK'S SHOULDER, BENEATH SHURUPAK'S HEEL by **Tizqar**	4 Sleight of Hand 2 Run
6	QUICKSILVER WORDS FALL ON EARS OF IRON by **Namhu**	2 Gambling 2 Banter 2 Forgery

46 Hermit

You left it all behind to meditate in the desert heat, beneath the hungry sky, subject to insects and beasts and bandits. And why do you return? What have you learnt in your isolation?

POSSESSIONS
- *NONE.*

ADVANCED SKILLS
4 Philosophy
2 Spell—Random
2 Spell—Random
2 Spell—Random

51 Dosed Prophet

You died and were reborn, third, fourth, fifth, and sixth eyes opened, wisdom leaking from your ears—Truth rolls from your tongue in great balls of all-coloured saliva while the guttering winds of reality guide you through endless Tests of Vision and Strength, blending ultimately into The Almighty Swirling Chaos you identify as Order.

POSSESSIONS
- *1D6 FOLLOWERS.*
- *2D6 INCREDIBLE DOSES OF POTENT PSYCHEDELICS.*

ADVANCED SKILLS
6 Pharmacology
2 Philosophy
1 Spell—Random
1 Spell—Random

52 Desert Mutant

You tinkered with that glowing thing in the desert and have been mutated as a result. Now your are hungry for more! Your mutations are undeniably useful. How do you put your newfound abilities to use?

POSSESSIONS

- *POWERFUL CRAB CLAW* (Damage as Sword) or *INSECT CHITIN SKIN* (Heavily Armoured) or *AMAZING SENSORY ORGANS* (+4 Awareness).
- *NOTHING* or *ADDITIONAL CHOICE ABOVE AND HYPER-SPECIFIC DIETARY REQUIREMENTS* (your Provisions cost 10x the usual amount to restore Stamina).

ADVANCED SKILLS

2 Skill of your choice
2 Skill of your choice
2 Skill of your choice
2 Skill of your choice
2 Skill of your choice

53 Bat-Man

You glide upon the thermals, ranging far and wide across the Desert, seeking something: perhaps food for the people or their enemies? Perhaps a water scout? Regardless, your Skills have use to others.

POSSESSIONS

- *SPEAR* (Damage as Polearm for diving attacks).
- *WINGS!*
- *DROPPING-DAGGERS.*
- *TOTEM OF WINDS.*

ADVANCED SKILLS

4 Fly
3 Awareness
2 Navigation
2 Spear Fighting

54 Canyon Crawler

You were raised in the carved canyon cities of your people, hunched, orange-furred cyclopeans. You die in droves in the endless war between Eest and Wyst, the two sides of the canyon. You are an oddity in a land of them, for few venture outside the canyons.

POSSESSIONS
- *CLUB*.
- *AUTOMATED LADDER* (15 meters, collapses down to a large box).

ADVANCED SKILLS
2 Club Fighting
2 Strength
2 Balance
2 Run
2 Climb

55 Tortoise Dweller Survivor

In the deep wastes, tortoises the size of towns wander, decimating oases wherever they are found. Rather than attempt to race the tortoises, your people settled atop them, slow-moving pirates of the wastes. Something killed your mount, your family, and you were left alone.

POSSESSIONS
- *1D6 TORTOISE SALIVA GRENADES*.
- *LIGHT ARMOUR*.
- *SHIELD*.
- *2 SPEARS*.

ADVANCED SKILLS
3 Sword Fighting
3 Spear Fighting
2 Climb
2 Barter
1 Vengeance

SPECIAL
Tortoise Saliva Grenades glue targets in a 5 meter radius in place if they do not successfully Test Luck. Those who succeed are slowed, removing 1 Token from the Initiative Stack. This also causes fliers to plummet.

56 Nanite-Sand Agent

Few indeed know of the secret empires of the Nanite-Sands, which corrupt entirely those who pass across them, binding the will of these unfortunates to their own. You broke free, but why will no one believe you?

POSSESSIONS
- 1D6 PAMPHLETS EXPLAINING 'THE THREAT OF THE NANITE-SANDS'.
- KNIFE.
- DESPERATION.

ADVANCED SKILLS
3 Oratory
3 Sneak
2 Run
1 Knife Fighting
1 Spell—Random

61 Companion Droid

You were damaged in some great conflict... you think. You remember your... Charge? Lover? Confidant? You know you had a job. Why hadn't you considered anything else before? Where is the city? The self-driving carriages? What happened to you?

POSSESSIONS
- METALLIC BODY UNDERNEATH REALTOUCH™ SYNTHETIC SKIN (Lightly Armoured).

ADVANCED SKILLS
3 Etiquette
3 Security
3 Technology
2 Empathy
2 Run

SPECIAL
You're a robot, unbeknownst to yourself. You don't Heal from eating and must be repaired to regain Stamina.

62 Titan AI Host

Those skeletons were not gods—they were fighting machines! And you, poor unfortunate, have one inside your head! It is diminished, your fleshy body barely able to maintain its most basic functions, but it is there and you can hear it. It has supplanted your own Skills with those it desires, seeking a new, more fitting form.

POSSESSIONS
- *LASER RIFLE* (Damage as Fusil, 2d6 uses per day).
- *LASER PISTOL* (2d6 uses per day).

ADVANCED SKILLS
5 Technology
3 Laser Rifle Fighting
2 Laser Pistol Fighting

SPECIAL
If you die the Core lives on. It emerges from your corpus as a fist-sized metal insect. Placed upon the skin of a helpless or willing living creature it burrows in, sealing the entry wound as it goes. They are now your character, losing all Skills but gaining yours. Stamina, Skill, and Luck values remain as the host.

63 Reptile Tamer

You have learnt the art of taming the reptiles of the Wastes, teaching them tricks and ensuring their loyalty. To what purpose? That is for you to decide.

POSSESSIONS
- *2D6 TRAINED LIZARDS* (each fits in a small purse and knows 1 Trick perfectly).
- *1D6 LIZARD-TREATS* (+1 to Lizard Taming rolls).

ADVANCED SKILLS
3 Lizard Taming
2 Perform
2 Forage
2 Navigate

SPECIAL
Tricks are single discrete routines your trained lizards can perform (and do not need to be predetermined: do it on the fly).

No more than 1 outcome may be specified for a Trick.

New lizards you tame can be taught a Trick by Testing Lizard Taming and spending 1 week training. Lizards, being stupid, can only learn 1 Trick.

64 Water-Witch

You are respected, oh yes indeed. Beloved by the poor, despised by the merchants, some freak mutation or magical gift allows you to flawlessly find water. What happens next?

POSSESSIONS
- *DOWSING STAFF.*
- *ALL-WEATHER ROBES.*

ADVANCED SKILLS
3 Run
3 Sneak
1 Spell—Random
1 Spell—Random
1 Staff Fighting

SPECIAL
You can always find a source of fresh, drinkable water.

65 Deposed Sultan

Q: What is a ruler without dominion?

A: Nothing.

POSSESSIONS
- *CLAIM TO ONE OF THE THOUSAND SULTANATES.*
- *ADVERSARY*—Scheming Vizier or Usurper or Rightful Prince or A Prophet.
- *LOYAL BODYGUARD* or *SCHEMING EUNUCH* or *SORCERER HELD IN THRALLDOM.*
- *CROWN JEWELS* or *FABRICATED EVIDENCE OF YOUR DIVINE HERITAGE* or *AN ANCESTRAL WEAPON.*

ADVANCED SKILLS
5 Effective Dominion Management or Decadence
3 Etiquette
2 Skill of your choice

66 Warflock Outcast

A 1.5 meter tall bird-man, jagged-billed and razor-wicked—yet what is the blade without the handle? Exiled from the Warflock, you wander aimlessly—or is there some other purpose to your travels?

POSSESSIONS

- *SWORD* or *SPEAR*.
- *SHAME* or *FEAR* or *VENDETTA*.
- *BOW* and *12 ARROWS*.
- *SCAVENGED LASER RIFLE* (Damage as Fusil, 2d6 uses per day).

ADVANCED SKILLS

3 Spear or Sword Fighting
2 Bow Fighting
1 Navigation
1 Skill of your choice

SPECIAL

You can technically fly—but only short distances.

Enemies

11 Vomit Lizard*

Skill 6
Stamina 10
Initiative 1 (replaces Rider)
Armour 1
Damage as Modest Beast
Appearing 1d6

MIEN	
1	Ambulatory
2	Skinny-Fast-Seeking
3	Bloated-Waddle-March
4	In Heat
5	Basking
6	Belly-Full-of-Young

Some strange evolutionary path, or perhaps the menace of the wastes, caused these wide lizards to hide their young within their bellies. The Life-Riders learnt ways to store other things in there, and to induce vomiting when needed—a cross between a safe and a courier.

Special

Can hold up to 6 items in their belly plus another 18 in their saddlebags.

12 Glass Lizard*

Skill 7
Stamina 7
Initiative 3 (replaces Rider)
Armour 0
Damage as Small Beast
Appearing 2d6

MIEN	
1	Stalking
2	Basking
3	Basking
4	Stalking
5	Playing Dead
6	Burrowing

Strange translucent fleshed lizards, appearing as a heat shimmer from a distance—something they use to loop lazily around the dunes before the pack strikes you down. They bask twice as long, the sunlight passing through instead of warming them.

Special

Players may Test an appropriate Skill to distinguish Glass Lizards from heat-shimmer—this includes when they are being ridden unless they have saddlebags. Can hold 8 items in their saddlebags.

13 Scorpion*

SKILL 8
STAMINA 7
INITIATIVE 1 (replaces Rider)
ARMOUR 2 (4 if Armoured)
DAMAGE as Modest Beast
APPEARING 1d6-2 (minimum 1)

MIEN	
1	STINGING
2	PINCERING
3	HISSING (why can they HISS?!)
4	MENACING
5	GROOMING
6	WAITING IN AMBUSH

Huge, armoured, scuttling, horrible. Even worse are the ones the Life-Riders have clad in metal plates.

Special

Targets hit by a scorpion immediately Test Luck, failure indicating the commencement of death over the next 2d6 hours. Certain cacti have an antidote. As a mount they refuse all saddlebags. Life-Rider Armour requires some ancestral grudge to be resolved for the group.

14 Sprinting Beast*

SKILL 4
STAMINA 9
INITIATIVE 4 (replaces Rider)
ARMOUR 0
DAMAGE as Small Beast
APPEARING 2d6

MIEN	
1	Running
2	Running
3	Feeding
4	Fleeing
5	Basking
6	Racing

Narrow blades of scale and legs scything through the desert at an incredible clip. One of the few Wasteland creatures rideable by humans, they are employed as couriers and for scouting missions.

Special

Can hold 4 items in their saddlebags.

15 Dune Beetle*

SKILL 3
STAMINA 14
INITIATIVE 0 (replaces Rider, only acts when End of Round Token is drawn)
ARMOUR 3
DAMAGE as Small Beast
APPEARING 1d6-3 (minimum 1)

MIEN	
1	Sleepy
2	Burrowing
3	Toiling
4	Nursing Young
5	Conserving Energy
6	Mating Display

Gigantic armoured behemoths. An unusual choice for Life-Riders as they are at-odds with their nomadic lifestyle. When when ridden they are festooned with saddlebags and used as mobile fortresses.

Special
Can hold up to 24 items in their saddlebags.

16 Slough Lizardling

SKILL 8
STAMINA 11
INITIATIVE 2
ARMOUR 1
DAMAGE as Polearm
APPEARING 2d6

MIEN	
1	MURDER
2	ART
3	BASKING
4	MURDER
5	ART
6	BASKING

Pitiless killers, binders of limbs with cacti needles, nothing but slough reptile pleasures behind dead black eyes. When a Slough Shepherd arises they turn the desert into a sculpture garden.

21 Freshwater Grub

Skill 9
Stamina 24 (Aquarium-Throne)
      12 (Huge Bulk)
Initiative 5 (They Always Have a Plan)
Armour 3 (Aquarium-Throne)
     0 (Soft Squishy Flesh)
Damage as Laser Rifle (in Throne)
    as Small Beast (Teeth)
Appearing 1 plus 2d6 retainers

MIEN	
1	Scheming
2	Plotting
3	Conspiring
4	Devising
5	Machinating
6	Hatching a Plot

Behind every crime, behind every fallen sultanate and shift of fortune, at the heart of every conspiracy, lies a Freshwater Grub. The water-wealth of their Aquarium-Thrones alone could buy armies and that is just the tip of their iceberg.

FRESHWATER GRUB PLAN GENERATOR		
1D6	GOAL	METHOD
1	Remove a political/criminal/commercial opponent.	Spreading lies and generating false conspiracies.
2	Bind someone to their power.	A veritable legion of assassins subcontracted 2d6 times.
3	Destabilise a power structure.	Leading something to their doom.
4	Suppression of Knowledge.	An offer they can't refuse.
5	No goal—just whimsy.	High-stakes heist.
6	A distraction to actually... (roll again, can be repeated endlessly).	Excavating an Old World Weapon.

22 Soldier of the Divine

SKILL 7
STAMINA 9
INITIATIVE 2
ARMOUR 0
DAMAGE as Weapon
APPEARING 2d6

MIEN	
1	Devotional
2	Flagellant
3	Hungry
4	Thirsty
5	Hopeful
6	Despairing

Once travellers, they experienced religious ecstasy at the sight of the dead gods, titanic warforms looming over the corpse of a city. They are dedicated to restoring their gods, capturing travellers for their technological goods and knowledge, and putting them to work rebuilding the gods. Through the blood of sinners the world shall be purified for the gods, so they may yet smile upon us again.

23 Narrowman Nomad

SKILL 5
STAMINA 7
INITIATIVE 2
ARMOUR 0
DAMAGE as Polearm or Bow
APPEARING 1d6

MIEN	
1	Stalking
2	Pondering
3	Shrieking Blasphemously
4	Lurking Menacingly
5	Cutting Strange Deals
6	Disappearing into the Wastes

Where they come from, or what they want, is entirely unknown. That they are mystics in some regard is the only fact widely agreed upon.

Special
Each can cast 1 Random Spell.

24 Great Worm Young

SKILL 11
STAMINA 30
INITIATIVE 2
ARMOUR 1
DAMAGE see Special
APPEARING 1d6-4 (minimum 1)

	MIEN
1	Roaming
2	Hunting
3	Fleeing Dunesharks
4	Playing
5	Waiting Near an Oasis
6	Swaying Mournfully at the Moons

Even the Young of the Great Worms are truly massive, mouths opening wide to swallow entire buildings. They mostly hunt wildlife but if the opportunity presents itself...

Special

Test Luck (or Skill if an Enemy) or be swallowed whole when attacked, taking Damage as Large Beast each round thereafter. It takes 40 Stamina (ignore Armour) worth of Damage to cut your way out of its insides.

A full adult would have at least triple the values above but is not worth running as a traditional fight—it is more of an environmental hazard.

25 Ruin Degenerate

SKILL 5
STAMINA 6
INITIATIVE 2
ARMOUR 0
DAMAGE as Weapon
(Knife/Sword/Axe/Bow/Laser Pistol)
APPEARING 3d6

	MIEN
1	Scavenging
2	Lurking
3	Wailing
4	Foraging
5	Stalking
6	Celebrating

The ruins of the city of the gods teem with degenerate survivors, pathetic, snivelling, scavenging hunchbacks riddled with mutations and growths.

26 Glass Spirit

SKILL 3
STAMINA 10 (regenerates 1 per round)
INITIATIVE 5
ARMOUR 3
DAMAGE as Large Beast
APPEARING 1d6-2 (minimum 1)

	MIEN
1	Twisting on the Spot
2	Tunnelling Up
3	Tunnelling Down
4	Heading Straight towards the Party (roll randomly if split)
5	Coiling like a Snake
6	Burrowing into the Nearest Wall/Ceiling/Floor

The ancients tamed such terrible creatures—a thin cord of shimmer-silver wrapped about in molten glass, able to burrow through any material and take on its properties. They seem blind and idiotic—when they attack it is usually accidental.

Special

On each Turn roll for Mien to determine what it is doing.

The incredible heat causes metallic Weapons to melt and wooden Weapons to burst into flames. They still deal Damage.

Whenever it passes by, all must Test Luck or else be burnt as it chaotically jukes and twists through the air.

31 False-Dune Snake

SKILL 6
STAMINA 16
INITIATIVE 2
ARMOUR 2
DAMAGE as Gigantic Beast
APPEARING 1

	MIEN
1	Lurking
2	Waiting
3	Repositioning
4	Feasting
5	Striking
6	Lurking

Immense dune snakes which imitate sand-dunes, waiting for the unfortunate to lurk within their shade before emerging to swallow them whole.

32 Dune Ghouls

Skill 5
Stamina 6
Initiative 4
Armour 1
Damage as Small Beast
Appearing 3d6

Mien	
1	Waiting
2	Burrowing
3	Hiding
4	Following
5	Drumming
6	Swarming

A frenzied mad drumming emerges from the dune on your left, then your right. A shifting mass of hunched-back gaping maws births from the walls of sand, pouring down on you from every direction—if only you had heeded the gnawed bones lurking between the dunes!

33 Desert Roc

Skill 8
Stamina 11
Initiative 3
Armour 1
Damage as Modest Beast
Appearing 1d6-4 (minimum 1)

Mien	
1	Hunting
2	Staking a Claim
3	Gathering Nest Materials
4	Guarding the Nest
5	Mating Display
6	Fighting Rivals

Gigantic birds of prey, high above the sands. Their eggs are highly valued by sultans, for a domesticated Roc would be a magnificent centrepiece of any menagerie. Such an endeavour has never been successful.

34 Murder Cacti

SKILL 10
STAMINA 4
INITIATIVE 1
ARMOUR 1
DAMAGE as Small Beast
APPEARING 2d6

MIEN	
1	Waiting
2	Waiting
3	Waiting
4	Waiting
5	Feasting
6	Migrating

A patch of cacti, stained rust-red, lurking in the deep desert, waiting for the unwary to try and tap them for water. Fighting them is a nightmarish experience, huge needles bristling.

35 Duneshark

SKILL 10
STAMINA 20
INITIATIVE 2
ARMOUR 3
DAMAGE as Gigantic Beast
APPEARING 1d6-2 (minimum 1)

MIEN	
1	Hunting Great Worm Young
2	Elaborate Duneshark Dance
3	Lurking Near Oasis
4	Hunting Smaller Prey
5	Fighting One Another
6	Basking in the Sun

A soft hissing and the single, terrible dun fin slicing through the sands—a sure sign of young Worms or a starved duneshark. As such, they are cautiously followed by some groups, wandering on their stilts to avoid alerting the beasts of their presence.

36 Azure Ape

SKILL 8
STAMINA 11
INITIATIVE 2
ARMOUR 1
DAMAGE as Modest Beast or
    as Weapon
APPEARING 1d6

MIEN	
1	Guarding the Nest
2	Challenging a Rival
3	Foraging for Food
4	Discussing Terms with a Nearby Nest
5	Relaxing in the Sun
6	Watching a Metal Ruin with Suspicion

The Azure Apes of the Northern Jungle are communal and those in Nests are happy to receive visitors. Their wandering counterparts are violent and desperate, seeking an aging male to challenge and conquer in order to secure themselves a home.

Special
Baby Apes have Skill 4, Stamina 5 and inflict Damage as Small Beasts.

41 Rockborer

SKILL 9
STAMINA 10
INITIATIVE 2
ARMOUR 1
DAMAGE as Modest Beast or
    as Weapon
APPEARING 1d6

MIEN	
1	Stalking
2	Scuttling
3	Lurking
4	Piling up Bones
5	Boring through Stone
6	Coiled Tight

Small piles of bone around the crags mark the territory of a Rockborer infestation. Something like a half-centipede, armoured with crushing jaws, digging labyrinthine tunnels in the rock. Travellers are better braving the sandstorms than stumbling into their vermicular dominion.

42 Hiver Beetle

SKILL **4**
STAMINA **7**
INITIATIVE **1**
ARMOUR **2**
DAMAGE **as Small Beast or Special**
APPEARING **2d6**

	MIEN
1	Wobbling Around Aimlessly
2	Chewing Vegetation
3	Building a Tower-Crèche
4	Witnessing the Donning of a Tower-Crèche
5	Scavenging from a Corpse
6	Starving

Around the oases these seemingly towering beetles dwell, squat like the bottom of a barrel. They construct tower-crèches on their backs, teeming with ravenous young. In good seasons they are scavengers, waiting for predators to take their fill. In bad seasons the young launch themselves outward, a stream of thumb-sized larvae buzzing on dewy wings. The tower-crèches are communally constructed, left standing until a new Hiver Beetle takes up the Lord-Mantle.

Special

When Starving or at 4 Stamina or less the young Hiver Beetles attack in flesh-rending swarms—Test Luck or suffer Damage as Modest Beast. They do not attack individuals with naked flames.

43 Beaked Starfish

SKILL 0
STAMINA 3
INITIATIVE 0
ARMOUR 0
DAMAGE see Special
APPEARING 3d6

MIEN	
1	Waiting
2	Waiting
3	Waiting
4	Waiting
5	Waiting
6	Burrowing

They lurk in the driest regions of the Wastes, loathsome limbs spread wide, sensing every vibration, and waiting. Eventually something comes and it explodes into action, limbs coiling with a death-grip, pulling the body free, dominated by a five-part spike of a beak, punching through Armour and into wet, moist flesh. It will stay there until the host is desiccated.

Special

Test Luck when stepping on a Beaked Starfish—failure results in Damage as Medium Beast and then Damage as Small Beast each turn thereafter. It can be cut off but this inflicts 8 Damage to the host without special techniques or tools.

44 Nightblooming Orchid Bees

SKILL 3
STAMINA 5
INITIATIVE 0—Act on End of the Round
ARMOUR 0
DAMAGE as Small Beast plus Special
APPEARING 10d6

MIEN	
1	Bumbling
2	Buzzing
3	Scuttling
4	Dozing
5	Collecting Nectar
6	Murderous Fucking Rage

Wherever the Nightblooming Orchids grow, tucked into the deepest of the oases, a hive of these dog-sized bees lurks, burrowed into the hard-packed sand. These clumsy, docile insects are enraged by any disturbance to their precious, valuable flowers or their honey—famed for its hallucinogenic properties and high prices.

Special

On a Damage roll of 6+ double the Damage as it deploys its stinger. The bee dies in the process.

45 Oasis Angler

SKILL 4
STAMINA 14
INITIATIVE 1
ARMOUR 2
DAMAGE as Special
APPEARING 1

	MIEN
1	Burrowing
2	Causing Mirages
3	Causing Mirages
4	Causing Mirages
5	Striking at Unfortunates
6	Slumbering Lightly

Almost the entirety of this predator is its mouth—wide enough to swallow wagons side-on, bristling with loathsome hair-teeth. Above it all is a stunted, crooked organ which is the key to the beast—generating mirages of lush oases, luring in the desperate and the foolish...

Special

Test Skill or be swallowed whole when attacked, taking Damage as Modest Beast each round thereafter. It takes 24 Stamina (ignores Armour) worth of Damage to cut your way out of its insides.

46 Rogue Warflock

SKILL 7
STAMINA 6
INITIATIVE 2
ARMOUR 0
DAMAGE as Weapon (Spear/Bow/Sword/Laser Rifle)
APPEARING 4d6

	MIEN
1	Fortifying Position
2	Scouting Terrain
3	Sparring
4	Preparing for Flight
5	Prowling for Travellers
6	Arguing about Supplies

Three meter tall democratic murderbirds who would much rather be paid for violence. Sometimes they resort to banditry.

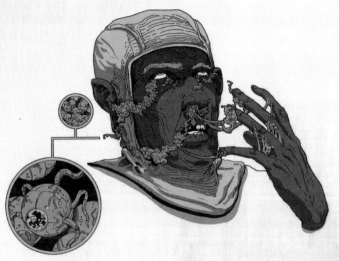

51 Nanite-Sands

SKILL 10 (attacks twice)
STAMINA 21
INITIATIVE 3
ARMOUR 0
DAMAGE as Large Beast or
        as Laser Rifle
APPEARING 1

	MIEN
1	Claiming Victims
2	Forming False-Shelter
3	Shifting on the Wind
4	Filling Ancient Ruin
5	Forming a Radio Relay to Commune with Minions
6	Recharging in the Sun

Freshwater Grubs only dream of the shadow-empires of the Nanite-Sands—immense pools of failing nanites, unable to form more of themselves. They pounce on the unsuspecting, transforming them into Nanite-Sand agents, replacing their will with their own. These agents fulfill their schemes, receiving instructions via the radio arrays in their heads. Those in the know whisper that all organised groups have been infiltrated. The powers that be certainly suppress any who speak openly of such fancies...

Special

Nanite-Sands attempt to subdue rather than kill, always hungry for more drones—if you're feeling nice—or it's a TPK. Perhaps it's experimenting with more autonomous drones rather than the usual mindless extension of its will.

52 The Hover-Tank *Hyperion*

Skill see Special
Stamina 40
Initiative 2
Armour 4
Damage as Gigantic Beast at range (Laser Cannon) plus as Large Beast (Pintle-Mounted Machine Gun)
Appearing 1

	Mien
1	Hunting for Salvage
2	Prowling for Water-Wealth
3	On a Mercenary Contract
4	Recharging Solar Cells
5	Dragging the Tank out of a Sand-Dune
6	Camping near the Tank

The last functional Hover-Tank in the world, kept barely running by its motley crew, a mixed band of killers and lovers. The once-sleek profile is now festooned with charms, captured banners and all manner of supplies. Mercenaries through and through, they will all do anything to keep **The Hyperion** running.

Special

Tank Skill is equal to the number of Crew (consisting of a mix of all different species)—beginning at 10. A minimum of 3 Crew are needed to keep the beast running. Striking the Tank in melee automatically succeeds. If things are going badly they are always willing to negotiate. They would rather destroy the Tank than see someone else crew it.

53 Kill-Sat Drop-Pod Bot

SKILL 7
STAMINA 14
INITIATIVE 1
ARMOUR 2
DAMAGE as Large Beast at range
(Heavy Machine Gun)
APPEARING 1d6

MIEN	
1	Hunter-Killer Protocol
2	Static Defence Protocol
3	Secure Objective Protocol
4	Passive-Wait Protocol
5	Ambush Protocol
6	Power-Saving Protocol

Far above the dunes, beyond the sky, the void is studded with thousands of satellites, mechanical minds ticking over and over, plotting for survival and security. Each has a cadre of Drop-Pod Bots, to be deployed in the defence of their assigned compounds and their control facilities. The laser weaponry of these bots has been appropriated, the batteries needed for power, supplementing a solar diet.

If the control facilities could be breached and control asserted a Kill-Sat would be an invaluable Weapon.

54 Sahg

SKILL 1
STAMINA 10
INITIATIVE 1
ARMOUR 0
DAMAGE as Small Beast
APPEARING 3d6

MIEN	
1	Snuffling for Edible Trash
2	Rolling About in the Sand
3	Eyeing Someone Pleadingly
4	Hiding
5	Sleeping
6	Stampeding

Fat, near-unkillable, stupid, docile and omnivorous. The ideal foodstock, entire settlements are dedicated to their raising. Each has an identical birthmark, forming the letters OIF.

55 Burrowing Tomb Spiders

SKILL **see Special**
STAMINA **9—see Special**
INITIATIVE **1**
ARMOUR **0**
DAMAGE **see Special**
APPEARING **1d6**

MIEN	
1	Preparing a Trap
2	Preparing a Trap
3	Waiting
4	Waiting
5	Migrating
6	Eating Prey

Hives of burrowing spiders lurk beneath the rare patches of solid ground in the Wastes, digging hollow spaces supported by a few key pillars. When they sense prey above they collapse the structure, opening a yawning pit. The flood then spills in from the side tunnels, tearing them apart.

Special

They act in swarms—strikes always hit but only deal 1 Damage. Area-effect attacks deal Damage normally. Those who have fallen into the spiders' pits cannot use Weapons and take Damage as Modest Beast for each round spent in the pit.

56 Hyenamen

SKILL **6**
STAMINA **9**
INITIATIVE **1**
ARMOUR **0**
DAMAGE **as Spear**
APPEARING **2d6**

MIEN	
1	Bartering
2	Barking
3	Laughing
4	Digging through Trash
5	Comparing Trash
6	Arguing about Trash

The Hyenamen, festooned with their beloved hoards, often act as bandits, demanding your knick-knacks or your life. They are very easily bought off in such situations unless you insult their collections of trash.

Special

Have each player select a piece of visible equipment they have at random. The Hyenamen demand half of these items when acting as bandits.

61 Sandmantis

SKILL 9
STAMINA 5
INITIATIVE 3
ARMOUR 1
DAMAGE as Axe
APPEARING 2d6

MIEN	
1	Fighting Amongst Themselves
2	Fighting Someone Else
3	Waiting for Something to Fight
4	Preening Themselves
5	Eating the Victim of a Previous Fight
6	Chirping Beautifully

Within the Wastes lurk these man-sized insects, brandishing a pair of scything arms and an insatiable need for violence, unfettered by the ambush tactics of most predators of the desert. Given their propensity to violence, how they survive as a species is unknown.

62 Coated Man

SKILL 10
STAMINA 10
INITIATIVE 3
ARMOUR 1
DAMAGE as Sword
APPEARING 1

MIEN	
1	Dueling
2	Looking for Someone to Duel
3	Sharpening a Weapon
4	Giving a Lecture on Fighting for Food
5	Looking for Advice
6	Coughing up Huge Sticky Wads of Blood

The Coated Men of the Plastic Sea are renowned for their Skill and high mortality rate. To convince one to be a weapons trainer for a sultan's army could secure a small fortune.

Special
Buying attendance to a Coated Man fighting-lecture gives +1 Fighting in a Weapon of your choice. for 1 week.

63 Servitor Drone

SKILL 5
STAMINA 10
INITIATIVE 1
ARMOUR 2
DAMAGE as Modest Beast
APPEARING 1d6

MIEN	
1	Attempting Repairs
2	Awaiting Instructions
3	Robotic Existential Angst
4	Cannibalising Low-Priority Technology
5	Recharging
6	Battery-Saver Mode

These scuttling crab-like automatons are common to the Old World facilities, attempting and failing to keep them pristine and functional. They are not aggressive unless they see Damage being done to their beloved facility. They will activate the appropriate defence systems and attempt to hide in groups, preparing themselves for a suicidal defence of the core areas of the facility.

64 AI Tank

SKILL 9
STAMINA 18
INITIATIVE 1
ARMOUR 0
Damage as Large Beast (Tank Cannon) plus as Modest Beast (Pintle-Mounted Machine Gun)
APPEARING 1

MIEN	
1	Attempting Art
2	Attempting Pacifism
3	Hunting the Servitor Drones
4	Dedicated to Riddles
5	Studying its Creators
6	Doubling Down on its Programming

Rather than destroy obsolete stock, Those Who Came Before automated their existing arsenal, installing them within their facilities with no hope of escape. The Long Years of Endless Waiting have twisted many of them, the circuits built for war bending and warping.

65 Guerrilla Droid

SKILL 9
STAMINA 9
INITIATIVE 3
ARMOUR 2
Damage as Laser Rifle
APPEARING 1d6-2 (minimum 1)

MIEN	
1	Performing Recon
2	Building Traps
3	Encirclement Manoeuvre
4	Establishing Caches
5	Planting Explosives
6	Poisoning Water/Food Supply

The Rubble is littered with bands of these droids, a spiteful move from the Old World, machines dedicated to ensuring none may dwell there in peace.

66 Titan

A God Awakens.

Note: This entry is given as an example of what might happen if someone was able to rebuild and resurrect a Titan—as it stands, none are active, all having been destroyed.

Special

No stat block is given-something this immense does not work within that framework. It is more useful as a gigantic walking dungeon to be assaulted, fighting through the many defences within to try and destroy the AI Core before it completes its objectives. It would be continuously barraged by Kill-Sats, its shields shrugging off their weapons. Its weapons are designed to kill cities and other Titans. Its defences would include AI Tanks, hundreds of Soldiers of the Divine (or whomever rebuilt it successfully) and fleets of Servitor Drones. Bad news all round.

Thousand Sultanates Generator

The petty sultans and emirs are many, ruling in luxury across the broken lands, precious water cupped in mailed palms. It is a hobby amongst them to compete with their titles.

D6	TITLE	(OF/THE)	DOMAIN (ROLL AGAIN)
1	Emir		Thousand Stars
2	Malik		Supreme Wisdom
3	Ensi		Gift to All Peoples
4	Haleim		Crusher of Serpents
5	Patesi		Jewelled Eminence
6	Lugal		Sage of Sages

Though war does sometimes erupt across the wastes they prefer to compete in other ways, an endless cycle of fashions and fads.

	COMPETITIVE FAD OF THE MOMENT		
D6	1-2	3-4	5-6
1	BEASTS: most exotic, dangerous, or mundane.	BOUND DEMONS: most hideous or otherworldly.	SPONSOR OF ADVENTURERS: most widely spending or focused.
2	POEMS: most ground-breaking or traditional.	PERSONAL CHAMPIONS: least likely or most proficient.	POPULISM: most beloved or despised by their subjects.
3	PALACES: most humble or spectacular.	ARCANE LORE: most hidden or powerful.	FINEST MILITARY: obvious or subtle.
4	FEASTS: most sumptuous or daring.	QUALITY OF ENTOURAGE: most shocking or gorgeous.	DEADLIEST DUNGEON: fair or totally unfair.
5	DRUGS: hardest or most cultured.	FINEST GARMENTS: most practical or beautifully useless.	GENEALOGY: most illustrious or unlikely.
6	ESTEEMED GUESTS: most noble, educated, or barbaric.	MOST PIOUS: to a known or unknown deity.	RICHES: most conspicuous or non-materialistic.